True Prayers
FOLLOW AND OBEY

*187 Powerful Prayers to Help You Heal
Through the Power of God's Word*

by Lacey Whittaker

Edited by Lil Barcaski and Linda Hinkle

Published by: GWN Publishing
www.GWNPublishing.com

Cover Design: Kristina Conatser Captured by KC Design

ISBN: 979-8-9859746-7-6

DEDICATION

I am dedicating this book to my core. Justin, Addie, and Liv, thank you for always being so patient and sacrificing so much to allow me to write and do what I love to do. Without you, none of this would be possible to achieve. I love all of you three.

I want to thank my ever-loving Jesus Team; without you this wouldn't be.

INTRODUCTION

In this book you will find 187 True Prayers. This is a continuation of True Prayers Book 1 and True Prayers 2: Hear Him Speak. Just diving in deeper.

Do you find yourself asking harder questions? Search me, teach me to do hard things, help me endure through growth and pain, deliver me from selfishness and pride, help me conquer and go against the grain of the world and what it brings. Help me surrender and pray.

Keep going and never lose faith. Thy Kingdom Come Thy will be done.

1

Keep going. Keep praying. Keep going. Keep praying. Keep going. Keep praying. Stop the enemy's lies and rise. Rise, oh rise, as His bride. Rise as His bride.

May His bride rise.

2

Perseverance wins the race. Bowing low helps us see Your face. Enduring brings mighty things. Surrender helps me obey. Peace floods me and tells me I'm bought. I have won because of Your Son, I have won because of Your Son, I have won because of Your Son. Heaven, oh heaven, please come.

> "Now my beloved ones, I have saved these most
> important truths for last: Be supernaturally
> infused with strength through your life-union with
> the Lord Jesus. Stand victorious with the force of
> His explosive power flowing in and through you."
>
> —Ephesians 6:10 *TPT*

3

Never let me ask for the easy way out. Never let me quit and say I'm done. Never let me take the road everyone travels but help me go the hard way with praise. Help me see I can do this by Your strength and grace. Help me see the hard way grows something deep in me, something I would miss if I took the easy way.

Give me the strength in the hard and appreciate the growth that was taught.

4

Deliver me, deliver me, deliver me from the evil I can't see that takes ahold and stores up inside of me. Deliver me from selfishness and pride, deliver me from all of it. Deliver me so I can see the light and the way. Deliver me Father, this I pray.

> *"God, deliver me by Your mighty name! Come with your glorious power and save me!"*
>
> —Psalms 54:1 *TPT*

5

Take it all away. Take it all away. Take it all away. All the shame, regret, and past offense. Take it away. Take those thoughts that linger and prey. Take it away. Father, please take it all away and out of me. Take it away so I can see and praise.

Take away all these enemies that prey on me.

6

Search me. Search my heart. Search my soul. Search my mind. Search my flesh. Search me. Make known anything not of You. Make it known. Make known truth. Search me. I shall repent. Search me so I can live.

> "God, I invite Your searching gaze into my heart. Examine me through and through; find out everything that may be hidden within me. Put me to the test and sift through all my anxious cares."
>
> —Psalms 139:23 *TPT*

7

Peace brings freedom, freedom brings peace. Peace and freedom are two things I seek. Help me let go and be free. Help me surrender and live in peace. This I ask, this I reap, when I believe You have given us these two things.

Your supernatural peace gives me the key to live in complete freedom.

8

Shine. Shine. Shine. I hear Him say, shine, don't let that dull over take you. Shine, oh shine, let others see you shine the light from within. Show them the light, the light that never goes dark. Shine, oh shine, that's His heart.

> "Those who are [spiritually] wise will shine
> brightly like the brightness of the expanse of
> heaven, and those who lead many to righteousness,
> [will shine] like the stars forever and ever."
>
> –Daniel 12:3 *AMP*

9

Deep breaths and smile today. Deep breaths and smile today. Deep breaths and smile today. Deep breaths and smile today. Deep breaths and smile today. Deep breaths and smile today. Deep breaths and smile today. Deep, deep, deep breaths and smile today. You are loved from the deep of the deep, loved and always He will keep. Loved, tried and true, loved and He will honor you.

Take a deep, deep breath in and out. Smile.

10

Careless living, careless thoughts, careless habits, careless ways. Help us, Father. Shake, shake, shake. Wake us up to live in intent. Help us live for You, help us repent.

"If you are slack (careless) in the day of distress,
Your strength is limited."

–Proverbs 24:10 *AMP*

11

Work. Work. Work. You have called us to work. Father, let us work with pure hearts as we work for You. Lord, help us work and honor You with all we do. Help us work and speak the truth. Work, You have called us to do. Let us not miss this work You have called us to do. Help us to always work and glorify You.

> "They profess to know God [to recognize and be acquainted with Him], but by their actions they deny and disown Him. They are detestable and disobedient and worthless for good work of any kind."
>
> –Titus 1:16 *AMP*

12

Endure. Endure. Endure. Endure. Hard times will come. Endure and be strong. Hard times will come. Look up. Look up. Hard times will come. Endure. Be strong. Hard times will come. Grow from the hard. Press in. Push through. Endure and help us be more like You.

"But he who endures to the end shall be saved."
—Matthew 24:13 *NKJV*

13

Kindness. You ask us to be kind. You ask us to be kind. You ask us to be kind. Why is it so hard to be kind sometimes? Help us to see, kindness is You in me.

> *"She opens her mouth with wisdom, and on her tongue is the law of kindness."*
> —Proverbs 31:26 *NKJV*

14

Faith. Faith. Faith. Help me live by faith. Help me to see and believe. Help me, Father when my faith runs weak, help me Father have faith to dream, have faith to believe in the unseen.

> *"Now faith is the substance of things hoped for, the evidence of things not seen."*
>
> –Hebrews 11:1 *NKJV*

15

Help my spirit to long for You. Help my spirit to praise and adore You. Help my spirit to seek You above all things. Help my spirit connect with Your power and grace. Help my spirit. Help it stay alive in truth. Battle and win in faith, Father. Today, just help my spirit always to stay in Your will. Father, help my spirit to surrender and feel.

> *"Let my passion for life be restored, tasting joy in every breakthrough You bring to me. Hold me close to You with a willing spirit that obeys whatever You say."*
>
> —Psalms 51:12 *TPT*

16

Heal my heart. Heal my pain. Take this all and throw it away. I don't want to feel. I don't want to be sad. I know one day this heart will be glad. Take it from me. Please, oh please, take it from me. I need a key. Take it from me. I've never hurt this way. Take it from me. Hold me until it leaves.

Take this pain Lord, take it away.

17

Jesus. Jesus, come and take this away. Jesus, oh Jesus, I have never felt as I did today. Jesus. Jesus, may I awake and see a new day has dawned and You came to rescue me from all this hurt, sadness and pain. From all this, I kept tucked and hidden away. Jesus, oh Jesus, tomorrow when I awake may I see in a whole new way.

> "A new song for a new day rises up in me every time I think about how He breaks through for me! Ecstatic praise pours out of my mouth until everyone hears how God has set me free. Many will see His miracles; they'll stand in awe of God and fall in love with Him!"
>
> —Psalms 40:3 *TPT*

18

Father, do You hear me when I cry? Do You know my deepest pain? Do You hear me? See me through all of this and say child, oh child, I will never leave or forsake. Child, oh child, just let go today. Be free. Be free. Be totally free. I know you don't see, but please trust in me.

> "Rescue yourself from future pain and be free from it once and for all. You'll be so relieved that you did!"
>
> —Proverbs 6:5 *TPT*

19

Seek and save the lost. Save the lost. Save the lost. Save the lost. Preach His word. Love when it hurts. Seek the lost. Heaven come show us how to all be one.

> "But Christ proved God's passionate love
> for us by dying in our place while we were
> still lost and ungodly!"
>
> –Romans 5:8 *TPT*

20

Habits. Habits. The good ones and bad. Habits, oh habits. You come not planned to break them, set them, make them rule. Oh, how these habits have a hold on you. Help me, Father, repent and see. Help me break them and make good ones. Believe. Oh, I believe only You can make these habits a good thing. Help me, Father, see. Help me believe. Oh, help me, Father, help see the real thing.

> "Don't copy the behavior and customs of this world, but let God transform you into a new person by changing the way you think. Then you will learn to know God's will for you, which is good and pleasing and perfect."
>
> –Romans 12:2 *NLT*

21

Trust me. Follow me, He says. I will guide. I will provide. I will love. I will give your hearts delight. Trust me in this. Trust me with your gifts. Trust me then. Trust me now, sweet, oh sweet, children. Always remember to bow.

"No matter what, I'll trust in You to help me. Nothing will stop me from praising You to magnify Your glory!"

—Psalms 71:14 *TPT*

22

I hear Him saying over and over, stay up, stay up, stay up, you are almost there. Stay up. Stay up. Stay up. Stay up. Stay up. Stay up. Stay up. Stay up. Stay up, you are almost there. Stay up. Stay up. Stay up, you are almost there. Stay up. Stay up. Stay up. If you could only see where I am taking you. If you could only see it won't be long. Stay up, child, be strong.

Stay up. Keep your head above the water. The battle won't last forever.

23

Strong and able. Strong and kind. Strong and willing to stay in the vine. Strong as an ox. Strong as a king. Strong can mean so many things. May I draw my strength from You. May I never lose sight of You. Strong, I will be when Your presence and strength is all I need.

> "In conclusion, be strong in the Lord [draw your strength from Him and be empowered through your union with Him] and in the power of His [boundless] might."
>
> —Ephesians 6:10 *AMP*

24

I fought; I have won. I have fought, I have lost. I have fought but what am I fighting for? Aren't I only to be still? Don't You fight for me? Protect me. Guide me. Lead me. Help me surrender. Help me surrender it all up. My health, this sickness that stays. Help me surrender it up. Help me. This thorn in my side, I know too well. Help me come out of this pit I am sitting in that seems like hell. Help me. Take my hand. Pull me up so I can see that You were always right there standing fighting with me.

"Be still, and know that I am God; I will be exalted among the nations, I will be exalted in the earth!"

–Psalms 46:10 *NKJV*

25

Scream, shout, praise His name. He has come to give. Give. Give. Lay it down for Him. Say it. Declare this life I live is Yours. Take it. Have it. I want Your course, Your path, not mine. For when I walk, I walk in line with Your word, with Your truth. Lord, help me to always honor and follow You.

Let me honor and follow You all my days.

26

Go slow today. Very, very slow today. Go slow today. Very, very slow today. Go slow today. Very, very, very slow today. Don't miss the smile, the air, the beauty around you. Cast your cares. Don't miss the moment. Don't miss Him. Don't miss. Look up and see.

Go slow.

27

I hear Him in my deepest pain say, keep going through. Keep going through. Keep going through. Nothing will ever stop you. Keep going through. Keep going through. Keep going through. Nothing will ever stop you. Slow down your thoughts. Slow down your eyes. Slow them down, to see you are all Mine. Slow down. Slow down. Slow down. Enjoy the day. This is the day I have made. Slow down and see. Slow down. What this life is meant to be, will always bring honor and glory. Slow down. Slow down. Slow down today. Slow down and see me in a whole new way.

Slow down. Jesus was never in a hurry to go anywhere.

28

It's here. It's here. It's all here. I hear You say, it's here, it's here. Everything You spoke. Everything I've read. Everything You gave me. All my dreams. All my prayers. It's really, really here. I believe You died for me. I believe You love me. I believe that You give and I receive. I believe it's here and I will forever live in praise and thanksgiving, Lord, I believe.

> *"She said to Him, 'Yes, Lord, I believe that You are the Christ, the Son of God, who is to come into the world.'"*
>
> –John 11:27 *NKJV*

29

Steady and able. Steady and able. Steady and able. Steady and secure. Steady and secure. Steady and secure. Steady and sure. Steady and ready. Steady and ready. Steady and ready. Steady and ready. Steady and ready. Steady and ready. Steady and ready. Steady and ready. Steady and ready. Steady and ready. Steady and ready. Steady and ready. Steady and ready. Steady and ready. Steady and ready. Go now. Go. Go now. Go. Go now. Have peace. Have peace. Have all your wildest dreams. Go now. Go. It's time. It's time. It's time. It's time to shine. It's time. It's time. It's time to fly.

> *"For the Lord will act and carry out His word on the earth, and waste no time to accomplish it!"*
>
> –Romans 9:28 *TPT*

30

Worn spiritually, mentally, physically worn. Worn. It happens to us all. Hits us in the big and small. Worn. It comes on. Worn when we stumble and fall. Worn it's a familiar thing. When you trust in yourself and not the God who saved.

> "Are you weary, carrying a heavy burden? Come to me. I will refresh your life, for I am your oasis."
>
> —Matthew 11:28 *TPT*

31

I'm a winner because of who You are. I'm a winner because of Your word, Your truth. I'm a winner because I never gave up, I always chose You. I'm a winner because You died on the cross. I'm a winner because I am paid and bought. I am a winner. I believe this is true. I am a winner and I owe it all to You.

I win because of You Jesus.

32

Lord, I'm ready now. I've casted down all that held me back. All the fears and lack. Lord, I'm ready now. I was lost and now I'm found. Lord, I'm ready now. I'm ready and my mind is set free. My heart is able and willing to receive. Lord, I'm ready now. Lord, I'm ready now. Please send me, Lord. I'm ready now.

> *"God is our refuge and strength, A very present help in trouble."*
>
> **–Psalms 46:1** *NKJV*

33

Leave the past behind you. Don't live there anymore. Leave it behind. Learn the new is more. The past is there and now it's gone. Look to the present where you truly belong. Don't live back there. Don't fight. Just cast those cares. Don't live there. Move forward and see the present is where I'm asking you to live. Fully and completely in me.

Help me live in each day present.

34

Healthy identity is what I ask. To know I'm loved without the task. To know I'm bought and my worth in Him. To read this, is one thing, but to know this, I would truly win. Help me, Father, get this so deep. Help me, Father, feel this. You see, I don't truly know how much you love me, but I know, like I know, it's my identity.

Show me my true identity is only found in You.

35

Forgiveness is key. It unlocks grief, insecurity, pain and regret. Forgiveness takes place for us to live in a place of love, kindness, joy and everlasting peace. Yes, He died to set us free and tells us to live in peace. To forgive and be forgiven. To love the unlovable. To share grace just as our loving Father gives grace. Help me, Father, to forgive with your eyes and heart and repent without harsh.

"bearing with one another, and forgiving one another, if anyone has a complaint against another; even as Christ forgave you, so you also must do."

–Colossians 3:13 *NKJV*

36

Peace. It is impossible to have peace when expecting perfection. Why is this so hard? Why do I yearn for perfection when I know perfection was You, only You? Help me let go of perfection and live a life of peace and resurrection.

> "but when love's perfection arrives, the partial will
> fade away."
>
> –1 Corinthians 13:10 *TPT*

37

All the tears. All the pain. All the insecurities. All the rain. All the dark. All the cold couldn't leave me in that dark hole. All the prayers. All the giants. All the faith where I'm reliant. All the tugs to pull me near. All the love I felt. All the pride that was dealt. All the words He spoke. All the healing that came through growth, got me here, pushed me and sent me clear forward to where I am today. Sent me to His grace. I am forever changed. Eyes on Him. I'm ok. Eyes on Him. I can live again.

Eyes on Him. I am forever changed.

38

As the shadows grow dark, my spirit fades into worry instead of praise. Help me, Father, see the light. Help me see I am your true delight. Help me out of this fog. Help me over this log. Help me up outta here. Help me see again so clear.

> "Then she came and worshiped Him, saying, 'Lord, help me!' "
>
> —Matthew 15:25 *NKJV*

39

All this knowledge. All this strength. All this goodness You give to me. How could I want what this world offers me, when everything is given by the words You speak? Help me, Father, when I lose my way. Help me, Father, help me to stay in Your light, in Your way. Help, oh help me, Father, not to stray.

> *"Therefore, hear me now, my children, And do not depart from the words of my mouth."*
> —Proverbs 5:7 *NKJV*

40

I praise You in the valley. I praise You on the mountain. I praise in the middle. You are my only fountain. I praise You for who You are and what You have done. I praise You with every breath in my lungs.

> "For the Lord our God has brought us His glory-light. I offer Him my life in joyous sacrifice. Tied tightly to Your altar, I will bring You praise. For You are the God of my life and I lift You high, exalting You to the highest place."
>
> —Psalms 118:27-28 *TPT*

41

Life is like a blink. Why, oh, why I ask? Some things don't make sense. The hurt, the pain, the agony and defense. Lord wake us and show us Your love in the hard times of not understanding Your plans. I know You are always good. So, so good. Keep my heart there in faith until that one day I see Your face.

> "And now, O Lord, You are God, and You have spoken and promised this good thing to Your servant."
>
> −1 Chronicles 17:26 *AMP*

42

Moving on. Moving forward. Pressing in. Pressing through this. I only have the strength to do if You are asking me to move. Lord, when the battle is won, help me move along in strength and know You will be on the other side smiling and cheering me on.

> "This is my command—be strong and courageous!
> Do not be afraid or discouraged. For the Lord your
> God is with you wherever you go."
>
> —Joshua 1:9 *NLT*

43

Full of grace, compassion, mercy and truth. Full of grace. It leads them to You. The heart of our Father. So precious and true. Full of grace is all I feel from You.

Your grace overflows through the depths of our souls.

44

Life is like a breath. A pass of time, a wink, a close of an eye. Life is so precious, so why do we run? Why do we fight? Why do we go all day and never see the sight, the prize, the one at hand? How can we walk 10 miles and never know Your plans? Help us sit. Help us stay. Help us see Your loving face. Help us, Father, see this life is not eternity. We will be there one day, yes, but help us live our best before You take us home. Show us Your grace and throne.

> "But you don't have a clue what tomorrow may bring. For your fleeting life is but a warm breath of air that is visible in the cold only for a moment and then vanishes!"
>
> —James (Jacob) 4:14 *TPT*

45

We may never know what one act of obedience will do. Our yes, is our yes and by that we are blessed. Use us, Lord. Help us see. Our yes, is our yes and will always be. Take us to new heights. See us there. Help us show the world how much You truly care. Obedience? You ask and my answer will be yes. I may not understand but I know it's Your will, Your plan.

> *"But those who obey God's word truly show how completely they love Him. That is how we know we are living in Him."*
>
> **–1 John 2:5** *NLT*

46

Loving. I ask to be loving and kind. To cherish others as Your heart in mine. Loving and true. Loving. You have called us to be loving to our friends and foes. Loving all You can see. Loving. So hard to do, but loving comes from You. Help us love when loving is tough. Help us love others as You love us.

> "He has made His wonderful acts to be remembered; The Lord is gracious and merciful and full of loving compassion."
>
> –Psalms 111:4 *AMP*

47

I will praise You. I will honor You. I will walk in truth. I will obey. I will speak love and not hate. I will choose to lay all my burdens down. I will replace them and wear my crown. Know my worth. I will love one another and forgive. I will repent my sin. I will choose to see You. I will choose to set my eyes fixed on the good. I will live this life set apart as You have called me. This is my heart.

> "So set yourselves apart to be holy, for I am the Lord your God."
>
> –Leviticus 20:7 *NLT*

48

The strain. The tension. The heartache. The hurt. All that came tried to throw me off course. Sickness, unforgiveness, and pride. Wow. Felt like I could die when I look back. I wouldn't change a thing. Because of this, I have healed and grown. Because of the past pain, I now have new reigns.

With pain comes growth and perseverance.

49

Look up. Look up. Smile and believe. Look up. Look up to Him and see. It all is suddenly clear and I no longer fear. Look up. Look up. Look up and let those tears fall into a loving Fathers heart. Let Him have them all. Look up.

> "I look up to the mountains and hills, longing for God's help. But then I realize that our true help and protection is only from the Lord, our Creator who made the heavens and the earth."
>
> —Psalms 121:1-2 *TPT*

50

Peace, love and all these things seen and unseen. I believe in heavenly dreams. I reap. I sow. I reap. I sow. I reap. I sow all good things.

"Sow for yourselves righteousness;
Reap in mercy; Break up your fallow ground,
For it is time to seek the Lord,
Till He comes and rains righteousness on you."

–Hosea 10:12 *NKJV*

51

Loss is so hard and comes at a cost. It comes, and shakes, and rattles, and quakes. It hurts. It causes pain. Loss is something we will all endure. Something we are promised in this world. When you go through loss, you can choose to lose or look to your Heavenly Father that loves and adores you. Find strength in Him. It's the only thing that will do. He will give you peace and wipe away those blues. In this world, we will have loss, but when the One that comes that saved us from it all, there will be no more sickness, no more pain, only love, joy and glory in that day.

Oh, I pray for that one sweet day.

52

Broken. Tired. Ready to give up, that's what the enemy loves. He beats us down into a pit, then shoves us, shuts the door and kicks us in. Why does it take to get to the bottom to ask for help? Why, Father, does it take so long to yell? Help us out of this hole. See us there and take hold. We love You and know You can do all things. Help us see and forgive, not fall asleep.

> *"With God's help we will prevail with might and power. And with God's help we'll trample down our every foe!"*
>
> —Psalms 108:13 *TPT*

53

The hope of Christmas is for all, not one. The hope for Christmas is all here and for one to hope in such a glorious way. To hope for something else, for a change. This life we see with our carnal eyes. This life we see is no lullaby, so choose to hope. This Christmas Day hope in the One that was sent to save.

> "Now may God, the fountain of hope, fill you to overflowing with uncontainable joy and perfect peace as you trust in Him. And may the power of the Holy Spirit continually surround your life with his super-abundance until you radiate with hope!"
>
> —Romans 15:13 *TPT*

54

Mad. Angry. Lost. Confused. Oh, how easy it is to lose when things don't go your way, when others are winning and you are staying. Father, help our eyes to only see the plans and glory You have for me.

> "For I've kept my eyes focused on His righteous
> words, and I've obeyed everything that
> He's told me to do."
>
> —Psalms 18:22 *TPT*

55

Failures and disbelief. Try so hard and wake up grieving. Where did this go so bad? Where? When our hearts are to be glad, do we put so much faith in ourselves to do it all and never ask for help? He is the one that gives us strength. The One that holds our peace when life gets hard and you wear thin. Look up and begin with Him.

He conquered it all. We win.

56

Give me Your eyes. Give me Your sight. Give me Your ways, Your hearts delight. My want is to please You, to know You, to show You to others and care, to be the one that casts all my burdens, worries and cares. Take my hand, fill me up. Help me overflow from Your loving cup. Bless me, Lord, help me see this life I live is only to please.

> *"I am your servant; deal with me in unfailing love, and teach me Your decrees."*
>
> –Psalms 119:124 *NLT*

57

Bitter. Jealousy and hate. All this world and more. All this world. How did we go this far? Reach out and look within. Reach out, smile and win. Don't look to others for your worth. Don't look to others. Look to Him, the One who wins.

Turn your cheek, look to Him, smile and win.

58

Demons tremble and shake. They bow down at the mention of His name. I will choose to say Jesus come. You are the only way. Miracles come when we proclaim Jesus. You are the only way.

> "and to have authority and
> power to cast out demons."
>
> —Mark 3:15 *AMP*

59

Turn around. You have gone too far. Turn around. I'm here in the dark. Turn around. I'm still here. Turn around. Don't run in fear. Turn around. You missed the mark. Turn around out of the dark. Turn around. The light has shown. Turn around and child, come home.

> *"Don't be impressed with your own wisdom.*
> *Instead, fear the Lord and turn away from evil."*
> **–Proverbs 3:7 NLT**

60

Speak truth. Obey. Listen. Speak truth. It's a given. Speak truth. Obey and see what He does for you and for me. He wants only the best for us, that's why He says obey. It's not for lack or anything else, it's for our health, our life His way. So, when He speaks, choose to obey. Lay the rest down and see how He slays.

Speak truth and obey His word.

61

He's coming. He's coming. He's coming back soon. He's coming. He's coming. Where will you be? Will you be ready and bended on knee? Be ready. He is coming for you. Be ready. He is coming back soon.

> *"Then two men will be in the field: one will be taken and the other left."*
> —Matthew 24:40 *NKJV*

62

Lost, lonely, scared in a world, surrounded by I don't cares. Where did we go wrong? Where did we not see the throne? How did we get into this mess? How did we go and live like nothing is left? Where are all these hidden things? Where do they go and steal our peace? Awake us, Father, it's like a bad dream. Awake us. Draw us to Thee.

Help us see with eyes of faith.

63

Disaster hits. Disaster strikes from there. Do you cover? Do you hide? Where do you go when havoc finds you? Do you run in fear and hide from truth? Where do you go when you get hit the hardest blow? Where do you hide when your world collides? Do you run from sin or sit and loathe? Do you ask for Jesus to come take and hold? Where do you go when the hardest comes true? Do you cope with sin or Jesus and truth?

> " 'I speak eternal truth,' Jesus said.
> 'When you sin, you are not free. You've become a
> slave in bondage to your sin.' "
>
> –John 8:34 *TPT*

64

Disappointment, lack of trust, unbelief, tired and unloved. Hit a wall trying so hard. Hit a wall why didn't You call? Why didn't You call, wake me up and say look, child, all you have to do is lay, lay, lay all those heavy burdens down. Lay them at My feet and turn back around. My time. It is My time now. Repent. Go deeper and see that this life is really only you and me.

Wake me up when I fall asleep.

65

Mercy. Mercy. Scream and shout. Mercy. Mercy. His mercy pours out. Mercy and truth. Love and you. Mercy, oh, mercy how I see. Mercy. Mercy at His feet.

*"Great is His faithfulness; His mercies
begin afresh each morning."*
—Lamentations 3:23 *NLT*

66

The wind. So fierce. So strong, like a gushing force coming in a direction you cannot tell. A direction only from heaven, not hell. The gush of wind so strong and depend. The gush of wind comes to cleanse, wake me up from all my sins, blow through the caverns of my soul. Blow through and take away all the unknown. Blow through like a mighty wave. Blow through and take away and help me see from eyes of faith.

*"He spoke, and the winds rose,
stirring up the waves."*

–Psalms 107:25 *NLT*

67

Hate and discriminate is all we seem to hear. Aren't we all children of the One who saved? Aren't we all together in our faith? Why the separation and despair? Why the criticism and all the unfairs? Why does everyone seem to have an opinion or at war? Where is the love that was paid for? I pray the blinders come off. I pray it comes without a cost of separation and division, but for one to love another and be forgiven.

> *"But instead, be kind and affectionate toward one another. Has God graciously forgiven you? Then graciously forgive one another in the depths of Christ's love."*
>
> –Ephesians 4:32 *TPT*

68

Shake them. Shake them until they awake from the grave. Shake them. It's not too late. Shake them. You come to save. Shake them. Show them truth. Show them. You show them, Father, what they need. Show them Your ever-loving grace and victory.

> "Yahweh is King over all! Everyone trembles in awe before Him. He rules enthroned between the wings of the cherubim. So let the earth shake and quake in wonder before Him!"
>
> —Psalms 99:1 *TPT*

69

Victory. Victory. Everlasting victory. Victory. Victory. Everlasting victory. Victory. Everlasting victory. Rejoice. Rejoice. Rejoice. A new day has set. Lift, oh, lift that weary head. Rejoice. Rejoice. It's the end. Rejoice. Rejoice and live again.

> *"Yet even in the midst of all these things, we triumph over them all, for God has made us to be more than conquerors, and His demonstrated love is our glorious victory over everything!"*
>
> —Romans 8:37 *TPT*

70

Speak kindly you say. Don't be offended or go astray when others come to take a stab. Let go and ask of My hand. I will help you along the way sweet child. Pray. Pray. Pray.

> "Because the Sovereign Lord helps me, I will not be disgraced. Therefore, I have set my face like a stone, determined to do His will. And I know that I will not be put to shame."
>
> —Isaiah 50:7 *NLT*

71

Lord, give me Your eyes to see. Give me Your eyes to see. Wipe out my disbelief, my judgment and fear. Wipe it out. Give me eyes that care, that see the best, that never worries or lusts. Give me those eyes of peace, those eyes of victory.

> "Smile on me, Your loving servant. Instruct me in what is right in Your eyes."
>
> —Psalms 119:135 *TPT*

72

This world seems full of hate. Is it my eyes or really the case? When did we all decide to fight and come against? When did we think or feel we have to win? This is evil. I feel this evil run to hell. We will not bow down to your wicked ways. We will stand up and hear our Father say, My kingdom come, My will be done on earth, as it is in heaven. We shall praise His name. Shout and say, I believe in this way, evil flee. Now it's time to pray.

The enemy loves to conquer and divide. Show us Father how we can live aligned.

73

How long before I break? How long before it's too late? How long do I feel astray? How long before you come and save? I am my own worst enemy. These thoughts. These things take me down so deep. They take me down until I weep. Where did I make the wrong turn? Where did I go wrong? Wake me up and help me see these trials and temptations are meant to strengthen me.

In these trials in life Lord, I need Your strength.

74

Sickness. I battle a lot. Sickness was paid and bought. Sickness. Why do you rear your ugly head? Sickness. You torment. Sickness. You are sick to me. Sickness. I ask you to flee. Sickness. Don't come back for me. Sickness. My Father holds the key.

Father, I plead unlock this sickness for me.

75

Glory be. Glory to our King. Glory. Glory. Glory. Full of glory, honor and truth. What a King we serve. It's true. Honor. Glory. All this we see. Honor and glory. Our precious Lord, King. Glory. Glory. Glory all over You. Glory. Glory. Glory. Running wild and true. Honor. Honor. Honor. I surely honor You. Glory. Heavenly Father, glory to You.

> *"Pray like this: 'Our Beloved Father, dwelling in the heavenly realms, may the glory of Your name be the center on which our lives turn.'"*
>
> –Matthew 6:9 *TPT*

76

Broken hearts. Broken stories and lives. Broken dreams. Brokenness. You call us to be broken so we can receive, receive, receive and open up. Only our Father can come in and heal us. Open. Open. An open vessel I am, Father, when I'm broken. Come take my hand.

> *"Lord, because I am Your loving servant, You have broken open my life and freed me from my chains."*
> —Psalms 116:16 *TPT*

77

Begging. Pleading. Misleading. You see all comes from within. Your enemies scheme. Cast him down. Shut him out. You have a Father that knows all about. Don't let him steal another day. Rise up, I say.

> "Rise up and help me, Yahweh! Come and save me, God! For You will slap them in the face, breaking the power of their words to harm me."
>
> —Psalms 3:7 *TPT*

78

Grace. All this grace. Help me share the grace You give, the grace I see. Help me, Father, to be graceful indeed.

> "For by grace You have been saved by faith.
> Nothing You did could ever earn this salvation,
> for it was the love gift from God that brought us to
> Christ!"
>
> —Ephesians 2:8 *TPT*

79

Awaken them, Lord. Awaken them to truth. Awaken them, Lord. Why can't they see You? Is it the road they walk? The will they choose? Awaken them, Lord. It's only YOU.

Awaken us Lord to see You.

80

This is a short life lived on this earth. A very short life. I have heard a short life. I say a short life. I pray to end this life, looking up, hearing Him say, job well done. You lived humble and true. You lived following me. It's true. Now go rest child in the kingdom of heaven I have made. Go rest and lay. Lay. Lay. All this for you. I hear Him say, job well done. Your time is here. Now hip, hip, hooray.

At the end, when I see Your face, I long to hear You say, "well done good and faithful servant, well done."

81

The path. The path. The narrow way. Oh, how I love to stay. I have peace. I have joy and understanding. I have this path. I will never leave. Show me more. Show me the way. Show me, Lord, and when I pray take me there. Take me deeper. Show me what You have. I'm a keeper.

"In all your ways, know and acknowledge and recognize Him, And He will make your paths straight and smooth [removing obstacles that block your way]."

–Proverbs 3:6 *AMP*

82

To think of what I could've missed. Missed it all for what? A life of selfishness and insecurity. I thank you, Father, for coming after me. This life I live now, I would never want to go back. This life I have is all You, and that's that.

> "My old identity has been co-crucified with Christ
> and no longer lives. And now the essence of this
> new life is no longer mine, for the Anointed One
> lives His life through me—we live in union as one!
> My new life is empowered by the faith of the Son
> of God who loves me so much that he gave Himself
> for me, dispensing His life into mine!"
>
> —Galatians 2:20 *TPT*

83

Goodnight, I hear Him say. Shut down those thoughts and lay. Take a deep breath and peace be had. Lay there awhile and let's chat. I love when you're quiet. You can hear me speak. Surrender it all and stay with me.

Your words are everything to me. They bring me love. They bring me peace.

84

Compassion. Reaching the lost. Compassion. Loving at all cost, even when they hate and degrade You, even when they say things that aren't true. Compassion was the cross. Compassion. It was bought. Forgive and be forgiven. Live and keep on living.

> "But instead, be kind and affectionate toward one another. Has God graciously forgiven you? Then graciously forgive one another in the depths of Christ's love."
>
> –Ephesians 4:32 *TPT*

85

When the days are long and the nights are short. When you feel broken down and ran off course. When life comes and hits you again. When all you can do is cry and then He comes and rescues you. He comes and shows truth. He comes. Oh, how He comes to love you. He comes, and for once you feel like you're the only one. He comes. Oh, how He always comes.

> "He trusted in the Lord, let Him rescue Him; Let Him deliver Him, since He delights in Him!"
> —Psalms 22:8 *NKJV*

86

Do you ever feel so far away? So lonely, so scared? Do you ever feel like you are the only one that even cares? Do you ever feel so deeply hurt? Do you ever feel you have fallen off course? Do you ever feel heartbroken and insecure? Do you ever feel mocked, abandoned and dead to the world? Let me tell you, sometimes you will. Sometimes you will get so low. Break down walls so He can enter in and pour out all His love into you. His truth. His adoration. His grace. His security. Your worth. He will show you in an instant if you will see these things He longs to do, if you let go of the past and choose not to lose, if you forgive, repent and turn to Him. Wow, oh wow, this is how healing begins.

Go to Him as you are broken and a mess and watch how He heals you from head to toe.

87

I sit here and look around. I sit here with no one to be found. No life. Where are you? No spirit. Dead to truth. The flesh. Oh, how it shows. The flesh that all of us hold. That flesh you have. To bow down in Jesus' name. That flesh you have. No control or sting. Spirit lead. Soul be well. Flesh, oh flesh, die right now.

"Let me emphasize this: As you yield to the dynamic life and power of the Holy Spirit, you will abandon the cravings of your self-life."

–Galatians 5:16 *TPT*

88

Child, let go I hear Him say. I know it has been a very long day. Child, let go, for when you do, I will show those enemies of your's truth.

> "Your Word is truth! So, make them
> holy by the truth."
> —John 17:17 *TPT*

89

The pain. The weak. The hurting. You seek. You call us to go after them, but they have a choice to repent. Help us let go when we do not see and not dwell in the things that displease.

> *"My dearest brothers and sisters, take this to heart:*
> *Be quick to listen, but slow to speak. And be slow*
> *to become angry,"*
>
> —James (Jacob) 1:19 *TPT*

90

Grateful heart. My heart sings praise. Grateful soul. I feel Your love flowing through my veins. The power. The victory that remains grateful for You. I am grateful. I was chosen to be a part of Your plan. Grateful. Jesus, what more can I say than thank You for living, dying, living again for my sake.

> "You can pass through his open gates with the password of praise. Come right into His presence with thanksgiving. Come bring your thank offering to Him and affectionately bless His beautiful name!"
>
> —Psalms 100:4 *TPT*

91

My eyes on You, Jesus. My heart, it's true. I may have flesh, but my spirit and soul You have blessed. My heart on You, Jesus. My eyes may wander away sometimes, but they come back and see it's You only. They see the light. My ears hear You, Jesus. I hear You. I hear the sounds of Your name. I praise. I hear the glory You are, Jesus. The words You speak, I keep down in my heart. In my mind, I hear You in my thoughts. Wow, I can hear Your ways. Nothing is greater. Nothing more true than You, Jesus, than You.

I shall live with a constant yield towards You Jesus.

92

Past. Regrets and insecurities. When do they come? When do they leave? The past is the past and this I see. You died to set us all free. Help us repent. Forgive our sins. Help us move past and never again shall we fall into a pit with no remorse. Show us, Father, keep us on Your course.

> *"For everyone has sinned; we all fall short of God's glorious standard."*
>
> –Romans 3:23 *NLT*

93

Teach us. Show us knowledge. Lord, not many yearn to flow and be stern. Sit us down and show us truth. Make us wise just like You. Help us grow. Help us know Your heart. Your will, I shall forever hold.

> *"Wisdom can make anyone into a mighty warrior,*
> *and revelation-knowledge increases strength."*
>
> **–Proverbs 24:5** *TPT*

94

Hope. Love. Faith. Patience. Kindness. Goodness of all things. Wow, how I love to hear that ring. Conquer. Win. Fight. Again, the battle is won and I'm going to finish. Finish strong. Finish humble. Finish again. Time after time. It's no different. Go to the cross. See Him there. Go to the cross. It's what we bear. Go to the cross. Forget about you. Go to the cross for the One that died for you.

> *"Then Jesus explained: 'My nourishment comes from doing the will of God, who sent me, and from finishing His work.' "*
>
> –John 4:34 *NLT*

95

Some things I don't understand. Some things I pray and pray again. Some things are hard to see. The people that are led to be, they will disappoint, hurt, and bring you down. But how do you respond when You, Father, hold the crown? Forgive. Let go and see again that plank in your eye is a sin.

> "And why do you look at the speck in your brother's eye, but do not consider the plank in your own eye?"
>
> –Matthew 7:3 *NKJV*

96

Hurdles. Marathons. Tribulations seize all these things that try to get the best of me. When does it stop? Where shall it end? I know You have a purpose and a plan. When the earth shakes and I can't sleep, when my mind wanders endlessly, wake me up, and then shall I see, this is not how life You made should be.

> "For the Lord God is a sun and shield; The Lord will give grace and glory; No good thing will He withhold From those who walk uprightly."
>
> —Psalms 84:11 *NKJV*

97

Dark alleys. Winding roads. Where does this lead? Where do we go? Why such trouble, agony and pain? Why this hurt and little shame? Why do we suffer? Why do we lose? Why, oh why, Father, when it's You we choose? You never said it would be easy saying yes, but here I am, Lord, giving it my best.

No matter how hard the road is Lord, You always have my yes.

98

Faults. Finds. Accusations and defense. Where does this come against all these men? Where do they think they can come and take? Why do they devour us and choose to stay in the dark and evil are their ways? Protect us, Father, show us how to sit and not be phased.

> "However, I say to you, don't repay an evil act with another evil act. But whoever insults you by slapping you on the right cheek, turn the other to him as well."
>
> –Matthew 5:39 *TPT*

99

Why do we run away? Can we just not face the day? Why do we run and hide? Why, oh Father, why is it so easy to stay at bay when problems we face rise up in our way? Help us see them as Your faith. To lead us with a purpose and plan. To have us know it's all worth it one day, to be in heaven forever singing praise glory in Your name.

> "For you know that when your faith is tested it
> stirs up in you the power of endurance."
> —James (Jacob) 1:3 *TPT*

100

Where do people go and hide? Where do they stuff all those lies? How does that pride go untamed? How does it go and not destroy Your name? Help us see. Help us hear. Help us go the extra mile with no fear. Tear those walls down. Break us to see this life we live, is only for Thee.

> "Then Jesus said, 'I am light to the world, and those who embrace me will experience life-giving light, and they will never walk in darkness.'"
>
> –John 8:12 *TPT*

101

When we doubt. When we weep, it's Your face I shall seek. Father, oh Father, help me see this is Your plan, not mine to be. Help me let go. Help me know. Help me repent and no longer live in sin. Help me not gossip or tear relationships down. I don't care what this world says or does, I only care that I know how You love. Teach me. Show me a new way. For this, Father, cannot stay.

> "Yahweh's Word is perfect in every way; how it revives our souls! Yahweh's laws lead us to truth, and His ways change the simple into wise."
>
> —Psalms 19:7 *TPT*

102

The sick in spirit. The sick in health. The sick are sick and we are dealt with hopeless victims that simply don't believe You hold all the miracles and everlasting healings.

> "Stretch out Your hand with healing power; may miraculous signs and wonders be done through the name of Your holy servant Jesus."
>
> –Acts of the Apostles 4:30 *NLT*

103

Life can throw you for a loop. Lots of tugs and tears and I don't give a cares. It comes to cut. To knock you down. Life comes unexpected and throws you down. Life comes and if you aren't ready, it will take you. Life comes but we have a bigger God to look to. Cast those thoughts. Say your prayers because when life comes, it won't take you just anywhere. No fear. No doubt, our Father has conquered it all. He has come to give us abundantly all great things. Hold deep. Hold near. When life comes, look up and smile. He is right there.

> "So above all, guard the affections of your heart, for they affect all that you are. Pay attention to the welfare of your innermost being, for from there flows the wellspring of life."
> —Proverbs 4:23 *TPT*

104

Anxious. Worry and fear. You come hit me out of the dark like a thief in the night. You hit me when I think everything is alright, then you take the whip and don't stop there. You take me out with no regrets or care, but once you take me down and I see the battle is won and you are only a thief. The Lord comes and floods me with peace. Never again will you beat me into a pit where I can't see.

> "The thief does not come except to steal, and to kill, and to destroy. I have come that they may have life, and that they may have it more abundantly."
>
> –John 10:10 *NKJV*

105

Hurt. Persecution. Rejection. Offense. Wow, oh wow. How it comes and hits. I take a step and one of you are there. I look to the left and you are staring at me. I look to the right and plead, help me. Help me, Father, to forgive and see this happened to You. Surely it will happen to me.

> *"So, I am well pleased with weaknesses, with insults, with distresses, with persecutions, and with difficulties, for the sake of Christ; for when I am weak [in human strength], then I am strong [truly able, truly powerful, truly drawing from God's strength]."*
>
> —II Corinthians 12:10 *AMP*

106

The lost in spirit. The lost in this world. When will they wake up and be heard? Is it ever too late, Lord, I wonder and ask sometimes? Our prayers seem like a hard task. Help us let go and see You through. Help us know, it's You they will choose.

> *"What man of you, having a hundred sheep, if he loses one of them, does not leave the ninety-nine in the wilderness, and go after the one which is lost until he finds it?"*
>
> –Luke 15:4 *NKJV*

107

The poor in spirit. The poor in flesh. The poor You say to clothe and feed. Help us, Father, to be Your hands and feet, to do and say. Be led and free. Help us, Father, it's all for Your glory.

*"Give generously to the poor, not grudgingly,
for the Lord your God will bless you
in everything you do."*

–Deuteronomy 15:10 *NLT*

108

Orphans and widows. You ask us to care. Since when did the world walk on and not hear? Lord, help us stop and pray and seek all those requests You ask of thee.

> "Pure and genuine religion in the sight of God the Father means caring for orphans and widows in their distress and refusing to let the world corrupt you."
>
> –James 1:27 *NLT*

109

Jealousy. Envy. Boasting and pride. Just another way for the enemy to conquer and divide. When will we stand up and see this is not the way life was made to me? Love and generosity. He asks, love one another. Don't be mad. Forgive. Repent. Go to the Father with eyes to see He loved and gave His life for us to be free.

> "Delightfully loved ones, if He loved us with such tremendous love, then 'loving one another' should be our way of life!"
>
> −1 John 4:11 *TPT*

110

The children. Helpless children. My heart longs, for I see them and know you love them more. Bless these children. Lord, bless them to see that they have a Heavenly Father looking down on thee.

> *"I will not leave you as orphans [comfortless, bereaved, and helpless]; I will come [back] to you."*
>
> –John 14:18 *AMP*

111

Pain. Where do you bury it? Where does it go? Do you toss it away and face the unknown? Do you soak, sit and carry on? Do you say, Father, take it and help me be strong? He did not say this life would be easy. He did say one day we would be with Him, so believe me.

> *"Look on my affliction and my pain,*
> *And forgive all my sins."*
>
> –Psalms 25:18 *NKJV*

112

Times change. People go away. The past becomes ancient and the present brings shame. The future is bright, but how do I get there? The future, He says, do not worry or care. Live in today. Respect. Love and share. Live in today. Cast your cares. Live in today. Brace yourself with truth. Children, oh children, our Father is coming back for you.

> "Jesus said to him, 'It is as you said. Nevertheless, I say to you, hereafter you will see the Son of Man sitting at the right hand of the Power, and coming on the clouds of heaven.' "
>
> –Matthew 26:64 *NKJV*

113

Days come and go. This one thing I see. One thing I know, Jesus, Lord, You never change. Always steady. Always You. Remain Holy. Dynamite and pure. You are everything. Out of this world. Come back. Take us home with You. We are waiting to see this glory come true.

> "Every gift God freely gives us is good and perfect, streaming down from the Father of lights, who shines from the heavens with no hidden shadow or darkness and is never subject to change."
>
> –James (Jacob) 1:17 *TPT*

114

Rules. Regulation. Religion. A bust. Jesus came and that's a must. Honor Him. See Him through. Drop the rest. He's waiting for you. A relationship you can have. The best friend you ask. Go to Him now. Surrender and see. He will be there and never leave you lonely or without peace.

> "Then what becomes of [our] boasting? It is excluded [entirely ruled out, banished]. On what principle? On [the principle of good] works? No, but on the principle of faith."
>
> –Romans 3:27 *AMP*

115

Peace. It comes and goes. Peace. You flood and show. Peace. You are so calming. Peace. I love to keep you always. Peace. Never leave my being. Peace. You are my reason. Come flood my soul. Peace. I have you wherever I go.

> "then God's wonderful peace that transcends human understanding, will guard your heart and mind through Jesus Christ."
>
> –Philippians 4:7 *TPT*

116

Joy. Joy. Joy is our strength. Joy. Joy. You will always be the safest place of my security. Joy. You come and you give me peace. Joy. You have a way of carrying me. Joy, oh joy. The joy You bring is better than almost anything.

> *"Be cheerful with joyous celebration in every*
> *season of life. Let your joy overflow!"*
> –Philippians 4:4 *TPT*

117

The spirit realm. Oh, how I love to move in the spirit. To be led in the spirit. To obey in the spirit. Kill the flesh. Listen, surrender and obey. The Spirit always leads the right way. Ask Him to live inside you and Him to show you truth. Ask Him to love and guide, protect and you will fly. Holy Spirit You have a home in me. Thank you, Jesus. I shall reap.

> *"Let me emphasize this: As you yield to the dynamic life and power of the Holy Spirit, you will abandon the cravings of your self-life."*
>
> –Galatians 5:16 *TPT*

118

Flaws. Imperfections. Self-hate. Body image. All those ideals and idols the world throws at you. Makeup, coverup, photoshop, crop. Where do you think all those lies come from that never stops? The enemy of course. He loves to shoot you down and throw you off course. He loves to pick a way at you. He loves to fill you with lies and not truth. Stand up to him and say no more, not today. I believe the Lord has made me this way and I will choose to celebrate His way.

"A tender, tranquil heart will make you healthy, but jealousy can make you sick."
–Proverbs 14:30 *TPT*

119

Love. Oh, love, how could you love a sinner like me? How could you forgive and see the best in me? This love, I will never understand. This love was all part of Your plan. This love You have for me is greater than anything.

> "But God clearly shows and proves His own love for us, by the fact that while we were still sinners, Christ died for us."
>
> –Romans 5:8 *AMP*

120

Rejoice and be glad. All the suffering was had the day He took our sins. Oh, how we could really begin. Rejoice and be glad we are saved at last. Jesus, oh Jesus, the cross You bore. You took these sins. We shall rejoice forever more.

> "Rejoice in the Lord always.
> Again, I will say, rejoice!"
> –Philippians 4:4 *NKJV*

121

Take a deep breath and out it goes. Take a deep breath in with the know. Take a deep breath. Exhale the sick. Breathe Jesus in. It happens that quick.

> *"I'm bruised and broken, overwhelmed by it all;*
> *breathe life into me again by Your living word."*
> —Psalms 119:107 *TPT*

122

Snarls. Rips. Tears and distress. All comes from the pit of a mess. Don't wallow or soak there. Don't let him drag you down into I don't cares. Don't let depression get the best of you. Don't get whipped and go for round two. You have a Father that died to set you free. You have a Father to pull you from your knees. Call out to Him and truly see. Call out to Him and never leave. This I know, eternity will be here in a blink.

> "Anxious fear brings depression, but a life-giving word of encouragement can do wonders to restore joy to the heart."
> –Proverbs 12:25 *TPT*

123

What are you chasing after? Truth or lies? What puts you to sleep? Peace or a lullaby? What do you run to and look to hide? Is it Jesus or all the worlds' desires? You will never be full unless you seek Him. You will never let go until you repent. Open up your hearts to love a new way. Open them up and lay, lay, lay.

"I lay down and slept; I awoke,
for the Lord sustained me."

—Psalms 3:5 *NKJV*

124

Hate. Fear. Anxiety comes from the world and lesser things. You could live your whole life and miss our King. You could be so busy and truly never see the one that died for you to believe. Stop, I hear Him say, chasing the world and all it takes. Stop. Bow down and hear Him say, I'm the only truth. The only way.

> *"Jesus said to him, 'I am the way, the truth, and the life. No one comes to the Father except through me.'"*
>
> —John 14:6 *NKJV*

125

Arrows. Darts. All come from the dark. Look out. Watch out. It comes with a bark. The battle is won. It was nailed to a tree. He died to save the lost and sinners like me. Repent. Down on your knees. He has come to give you life. Please, don't flee. Times get hard. Trials are long. They come and go and make us strong. Seek our Father. Down on our knees. Surrender today and live for our King.

> *"and saying, 'Repent, for the kingdom of heaven is at hand!' "*
>
> –Matthew 3:2 *NKJV*

126

Shun. Shun the Spirit says. You feel it's mean and not okay. Sometimes a shun is to protect you. Sometimes a shun is to shine truth. Shun you are you. Help me shun only when You ask me to do. Awaken their hearts and spirits too. Awaken their eyes to only see You. When a shun is sent, it's sent to move. Oh, shun you are you.

> "But shun profane and idle babblings,
> for they will increase to more ungodliness."
> —II Timothy 2:16 *NKJV*

127

When the snares come and the bombs go off. When your life stops at one drop. When you hit the floor and can no longer move, what do you choose? Self-pity, worry, doubt? Are you down so low you can't climb out? There's always a helper always a friend. Jesus, oh Jesus, come take my hand.

> *"Pull me out of the net which they have secretly laid for me, For You are my strength."*
>
> **—Psalms 31:4 *NKJV***

128

It doesn't always make sense to what the Holy Spirit will have you do. Sometimes it causes awakening and so much truth. Sometimes it shakes and casts out fear. Sometimes it's to help us grow and not steer. Die to self, spirit lead. You are the best and it's only You I shall seek.

> "For the flesh lusts against the Spirit, and the Spirit against the flesh; and these are contrary to one another, so that you do not do the things that you wish."
>
> –Galatians 5:17 *NKJV*

129

Perfectionist. They say I am perfection. The enemy's plan to take us down. To make us feel defeat. To make us live. To fully be all about our ways. All about our faults. Heaven come down. Perfection was bought. A high price. It is perfection. Oh, perfection. Only Him. Only our Father. How perfect He is. Only Him. Only Him. Embrace your flaws. Let go of your sin. Perfection. You never win.

> *"Your perfection and faithfulness are my bodyguards, for You are my hope and I trust in You as my only protection."*
>
> —Psalms 25:21 *TPT*

130

Plans. Do you organize? Do you plan? Do you worry yourself into an anxiety attack? What are mere plans? What do they do? Our Heavenly Father says take each moment, take each day, so, why do we plan our lives away?

> *"Refuse to worry about tomorrow, but deal with each challenge that comes your way, one day at a time. Tomorrow will take care of itself."*
> –Matthew 6:34 *TPT*

131

Journal your thoughts. Write them down. Make them obey the word, not the crowd. Go there and see. Be intent to live fully, not by the enemy, but by His everlasting glory.

"Bind them [securely] on your fingers;
Write them on the tablet of your heart."

−Proverbs 7:3 *AMP*

132

Do you feel His presence? Do you feel His peace? Do you long to know the secret place He desires you to be? Do you go there often or have you never been? Let me tell you what I have in a best friend. The one that is always there. The one that knows all your worries and cares. The first one that loves to celebrate you. The one that never leaves, even when you fell through. Ask Him today. Say, Jesus, will you live and never go away? You always have a friend in me. The best of best you could ever see.

> "And Jesus said to them, "I am the bread of life. He who comes to me shall never hunger, and he who believes in me shall never thirst."
>
> –John 6:35 *NKJV*

133

A new day has set. A new day has come. Do you know the joy of the One? Do you know the joy, peace and strength? Do you know how to live and believe? Go against the grain. Go against the fleet. Go to Him and seek, seek, seek.

> "What joy overwhelms everyone
> who keeps the ways of God, those who
> seek Him as their heart's passion!"
>
> —Psalms 119:2 *TPT*

134

Don't forget the past, the hurt, the pain. Don't forget the way He took you away. Don't forget how bad it was there. Don't forget. Hold on to your new way of life. Hold on as He shows you how to divide the past, the present, the future too. Hold on, He's carrying you through.

"Go ahead and give God thanks for all the glorious things He has done! Go ahead and worship Him! Tell everyone about His wonders!"

—Psalms 105:1 *TPT*

135

What do you feel? What do you think? What do you do when you feel down and cranked? Fall into a deep pit and soak in misery and pain. Do you know the one that calls you by name? Do you know to look up and pray? Father, see me here. Father, take these tears. Help me up. Help me out. Take me now. Don't live in despair. Call on the only one that truly cares.

> *"Give us a father's help when we face our enemies.*
> *For to trust in any man is an empty hope."*
>
> –Psalms 108:12 *TPT*

136

Highs and lows. The depths of your soul. Where do you go? Do you run to Him when things get dark, lonely or sad? Do you turn to your loving Father and simply ask? Do you ask of Him? Do you choose or do you go along in pity and disillusion? Where do you hide all your cares? In your heart, your gut or nowhere? Go to Him. The One that sees. Go to Him. The One you can believe. Go to Him. Turn and see He has you and will forever through eternity.

> *"Do not be wise in your own eyes;*
> *Fear the Lord and depart from evil."*
> —Proverbs 3:7 *NKJV*

137

Do you do hard things well? Does it punch you in the gut as you tell? Do you fear the Lord or the feelings of man? Do you believe and trust it's all part of His plan? I do hard things well. It wasn't always easy. It comes from obedience, after obedience, after obedience. Obedience actually gives me peace. To obey is to be one with thee. Stop, repent, listen, and obey. Watch how your loving Father will lead you away.

> *"But whoever keeps His word, truly the love of God is perfected in him. By this we know that we are in Him."*
>
> –I John 2:5 *NKJV*

138

Do you gossip? Do you judge? Do you live to play a part that no one does? Do you go the extra mile and not tell truth? Do you go heading down a path less used? Do you hear? Do you see? Do you even think to pray and believe? Your life is gone in a flash. Where will you be on your last? Sitting, waiting, hoping to see Jesus' face or laying in a pit of disgrace? Turn from your old ways and leave that old behind. Come to the One that made life divine. It's never too late to repent and change your ways. Seek Jesus and be ok. It's time. It's here today.

> *"I call heaven and earth as witnesses against you today, that I have set before you life and death, the blessing and the curse; therefore, you shall choose life in order that you may live, you and your descendants,"*
>
> –Deuteronomy 30:19 *AMP*

139

Is your worth in gold or what heaven holds? Is your song of despair or praise with Jesus everywhere. It's His name we share. Is your life a dance or of truth lived out as a second chance? Is your heart broken and bare or beating for the One that cares? Is your mind battled and bruised or are your thoughts taken captive and seeing truth? Is your voice tired, speaking ill things or are you taking it above, soaring in mighty ways? Tell me where are you? Are you half way in? You have to choose. Lukewarm, hot, cold, where are you now? Are you living in this world or for the Heavenly King that soars over the world's roars? Surrender now, bow, and ask Him in. Take this life of mine and let me live again.

> *"But because you are neither cold nor hot,*
> *but lukewarm, I am about to*
> *spit you from my mouth."*
> –Revelation 3:16 *TPT*

140

Be patient. Be kind. It all seems fine until one comes for you. Until one ignores and rushes you. Until you are overwhelmed and feeling defeat. Until you go in peace. Let me see, Father. Let me see when I lose my patience, lose my grip. Help me, Father, help me see that when I am patient and kind, it really blesses me. Do you ever get angry and angrier and angrier until you blow up and wonder where it even came from? Take a deep breath, shake it off and know we are in this world and the perfection we do not hold. Forgive an offense and the way you think it should be. Forgive. Let go, be kind and be free. Kindness is the easiest thing you can share. How would this world be if everyone dared?

"rejoicing in hope, patient in tribulation,
continuing steadfastly in prayer;"

–Romans 12:12 *NKJV*

141

Do you have a deep, dark pain? A fear? Rejection? Do you suffer with your thoughts and let them spiral so far out of control you look up in a place you do not even know? Are you numb, full of regret? Are you living with no depth? Are you falling deep into a pit? Are there feelings you have missed? Come out, I hear Him say. Come out, I have called you by name. Come out, I'm here to stay. Let go and let the rest fade away. Come out. Call my name. Come out of the darkness and stay. I am here and forever I will stay. Come out. It's me that cast the other away. Let go, seek, and praise. He is holy and here to stay.

"But Jesus rebuked him, saying,
'Be quiet, and come out of him!'"

–Mark 1:25 *NKJV*

142

Did you leave that old life but keep looking back? Did you regret most of your past? Did you get to this day only to say, well I've made it but only by Your grace? Can You forgive me, Father, I repent? Can You see me past all of it? I know You can, but I don't understand how You wipe it away with a gentle hand. You say, come to me child. Turn from your ways. You have sinned but now you are ok. Come to me. Drop those burdens and see I have given you life and to be free. Come to me. Leave that old life behind. Come to me. Drink this new wine.

> *"And no one puts new wine into old wineskins; or else the new wine bursts the wineskins, the wine is spilled, and the wineskins are ruined. But new wine must be put into new wineskins."*
>
> –Mark 2:22 *NKJV*

143

What's your deepest hurt? Your secret you hide? What's the pain that keeps you up at night? Where do you find shelter? Where do you run for relief? Is it Him or lesser things? Go to the Father that loves to hear. Go to Him, open up and be healed. He will take that pain away. He is Abba. The one that stays. Go to Him now in prayer. He will answer. He will care.

> *"Pour out all your worries and stress upon Him and leave them there, for He always tenderly cares for you."*
>
> —1 Peter 5:7 *TPT*

144

Are you lost, lonely or scared? Are you running this world dark in fear? Are you unsure where to start or even care? Look up to the One who knows you. Look up and say, Lord, I need You. Help me find my way to You. Help me see You are You. Help me to love and adore You. Help me, Father, I only want You. Let go of the world and what it brings. Go to our Father that shines glory.

> *"For the Son of Man has come to seek
> and to save that which was lost."*
>
> –Luke 19:10 *NKJV*

145

The truth? All the lies? Fake media and news? What to believe when so much is not true. You left us, Holy Spirit, to discern and see. You left us with wisdom to overcome these evil things. Open our hearts and minds to see truth comes from you, we know and believe.

> *"And you shall know the truth,*
> *and the truth shall make you free."*
>
> –John 8:32 *NKJV*

146

Do you struggle with doubt and insecurities? We all do. It's a real thing. Go to Jesus. Tell Him. He cares. Go to Him. He will find you there. Go to Him. Cast them down. He is the only one that holds real ground. Tell the enemy and his ways to leave you alone. He can't stay. Jesus, you are the way. Come. Enter in. Make a home and stay.

> *"When doubts filled my mind, Your comfort gave me renewed hope and cheer."*
>
> –Psalms 94:19 *NLT*

147

Are you lost, lonely and running scared? Are you going about life with no care? Are you choosing to live as this world or are you choosing to live for the heavenly reward? What will you choose? What will you give up for truth? Lay that old life down and serve the King that wears heaven's crown. Simply put, lay down your life and follow His ways. Glorify, sing, and praise. Today is the day.

"And what do you benefit if you gain the whole world but lose your own soul? Is anything worth more than your soul?"

–Matthew 16:26 *NLT*

148

Cast down those thoughts today. Cast them down and choose to pray. Those thoughts love to sneak in, but children, cast them down. You will win. Do your thoughts come like a thief? Do they come and stay? Do they wander? Do they lay? Learn to take them captive. Make them obey. The Holy One loves to say.

"Casting down arguments and every high thing that exalts itself against the knowledge of God, bringing every thought into captivity to the obedience of Christ."

–II Corinthians 10:5 *NKJV*

149

In this world we will have trials. He says, but take heart, I have overcome. I hear Him say He has overcome every trial, every sickness, every fear, every wrong doing, every lie, every care, every disease, EVERYTHING. Have hope. Have the glorious hope. He does what He says. He does. He loves. He loves. Go now. Have hope and dream. I say dream of heaven's eternity.

> *"These things I have spoken to you, that in me you may have peace. In the world you will have tribulation; but be of good cheer, I have overcome the world."*
>
> —John 16:33 *NKJV*

150

Today, I shall sit. I shall focus all my attention, all my adoration to You, my one true King. I shall sit, soak, and adore, thee. I shall conquer all my fears and insecurities. I shall sit and see this kingdom You died to give me. I shall sit and see all my hope and dreams comes from sitting still with Thee, today. I shall rise and sit. Honoring and glorifying Thee, today. Oh, today, how I missed sitting to say, I love You, Jesus. Never shall I walk away. Only to sit and hear You say a word, a thought, a dream. Oh, how I long to sit with You, my King.

> "There's a private place reserved for the devoted
> lovers of Yahweh, where they sit near Him and
> receive the revelation-secrets of His promises."
>
> –Psalms 25:14 *TPT*

151

Lord, help me fight. Help me win. Help me to see where to begin again. I'm lost, lonely, and scared. I need You more than I need air. Help me, Father, see. Help me be secure in all my insecurities. Help me look and see You. Help me behold truth. Help me when I fall apart. Help me with a brand-new start.

> *"I was desperate for You to help me in*
> *my struggles, and You did!"*
>
> –Psalms 120:1 *TPT*

152

Father, help my restless heart and my weary soul. Help me to let go of full control. Take me to a place where only I see Your face. Let me feel Your grace and be healed from head to toe. Thank You for peace, strength, healing, and dreams. Thank You for never leaving and always seeing. Help me push past and move on. Help me, Father, be so strong. Amen.

"So be made strong even in your weakness by lifting up your tired hands in prayer and worship. And strengthen your weak knees,"

–Hebrews 12:12 *TPT*

153

Lord, help me to take offense. Cast it down and not let it in. Help me to be tough and not take it to heart. All the bruises, cuts, and scars. Help me to remember when someone speaks ill of me, that it stems from a hurt within them and not really what they think or say to me.

"Don't be angrily offended over evildoers or be agitated by them."

–Proverbs 24:19 *TPT*

154

Father, Son, and Holy Ghost. I sure love You all the most. I can't imagine life without Thee. I can't imagine how I would be. I thank You for living inside me, showing me, leading me, and caring like You do. I shall live all my days praising and glorifying You in all that I do, all that I am. Help me to stay in Your plan, for I know if I am out of Your will, I will be backsliding down a dark stoney hill. Never shall I leave. Never shall I stray with You. No matter what I walk through, it all seems ok.

> *"Lord, so many times I fail; I fall into disgrace.*
> *But when I trust in You, I have a strong and*
> *glorious presence protecting and anointing me.*
> *Forever You're all I need!"*
>
> **—Psalms 73:26 *TPT***

155

Help me, Lord, when everyone leaves and breaks away. Help me, Lord, to say if I only have You, I have everything. May I not depend on them to get me through, but my Father that always loves and holds truth.

> *"You are my satisfaction, Lord, and all that I need, so I'm determined to do everything You say."*
>
> —Psalms 119:57 *TPT*

156

Sunshine on my skin. Sunshine, you always win. Sunshine in my soul. Sunshine, you always know how to brighten a day, how to lift a heart to pray. Sunshine, please don't go. Sunshine, you are in my know. Sunshine, you heal a heart, you touch a smile and that's a start. Sunshine, you are all mine. Sunshine, repeat and stay another week.

Sunshine you always win.

157

Family and friends, oh how it all begins. Some will stay. Some will leave. Some will be there when you truly need. This life. This life isn't always easy, sometimes unfair. I would say you grow apart and live different lives. Some stay in the world and some stay alive. Some go to Jesus. Some choose not to see the difference He has made and taught us to be strong. Holy, love and obedient. You see it's a choice and some will not make the cut. Some will run and do what they want. Help us, Father, to let go and see at the end of the day, if it's only me, I'm blessed by Your everlasting love and peace. I will survive. I will succeed, Father, if it's only You and me.

In this life, we live with so many people, Father. I only need You to see me through. I have, all I need, if it's only You and me.

158

Obedient. You ask of me to be obedient. It's a key, a key to unlock this path. The life I live. I'm called to be obedient in all tasks. I don't get to pick or choose. I don't get to. My yes is my yes. It's never questioned or doubted. I said yes to You and I will live everyday choosing You no matter how hard it may be, no matter how much rejection I see. It's You, Father, King of Kings. I owe You my yes for my life was saved on that cross. My yes seems so little to what You endured. Father, my yes will be forever Yours.

> *"And all these blessings shall come upon you and overtake you, because you obey the voice of the Lord your God:"*
>
> —Deuteronomy 28:2 *NKJV*

159

Send me Lord. Send me to the depths of the seas. Send me to the end of this earth. Send me to speak, to seek. Send me Lord. Send me. I'm willing, Lord. Send me. Send me. Send me wherever. You ask, I will go. Send me. Lord, send me now. Send me. Lord, I will bow. Send me. Lord, it's only You. Send me. Lord, You are truth.

> *"Also, I heard the voice of the Lord, saying: 'Whom shall I send, And who will go for Us?' Then I said, 'Here am I! Send me.'"*
>
> –Isaiah 6:8 *NKJV*

160

Simple. Simple. Simple tasks. Simple You may ask. Simple. Simple. Simple You are. Others make You complicated but I know it's not too far. Simple requests, simple ways to live. Simple. Simple. You chose to be simple with how You lived.

> "The unfolding of Your [glorious] words give light;
> Their unfolding gives understanding
> to the simple (childlike)."
>
> —Psalms 119:130 *AMP*

161

Father. Father, it's you I seek. Father, oh Father, help me to be. Help me to live for You alone. Help me to live and forget about my own. Help me to live each day as You see. Help me. Father, I choose to live for You, not me.

"and He died for all, that those who live should live no longer for themselves, but for Him who died for them and rose again."

–II Corinthians 5:15 *NKJV*

162

Shake it. Shake it off and run. Run to the Father that keeps holding on when life throws you everywhere. Shake it off and run to the One that cares.

"I say to myself, 'If only I could fly away from all of this! If only I could run away to the place of rest and peace.'"

—Psalms 55:6 *TPT*

163

You tried. You conquered. You won. You fell again. So very strong. Life will have ups and downs. What you choose, is where you will be found. I will choose never to lose. I will choose to walk these ups and downs with my eyes on You.

> *"Who is the man that fears the Lord? Him shall He teach in the way He chooses."*
>
> —Psalms 25:12 *NKJV*

164

Love comes and love shows. Love breaks hearts. Don't you know. Don't give up on this love. He died for you. Walk in love. Walk in truth. If everyone leaves and all you have is Him, you will know the greatest love heaven sent.

> *"There is no power above us or beneath us—no power that could ever be found in the universe that can distance us from God's passionate love, which is lavished upon us through our Lord Jesus, the Anointed One!"*
>
> –Romans 8:39 *TPT*

165

Cast them down. Spit them out. You gave them chances to show what you're all about. Cast them down. Spit them out. Chance after chance. Now it's over and out.

> "Then I beat them as fine as the dust before the wind; I cast them out like dirt in the streets."
>
> —Psalms 18:42 *NKJV*

166

How do we reject a word of truth? How do we say no and make an excuse? Don't you know this world will leave you bitter and cold? If He comes for you, run child and take hold.

> *"So, listen, my child. Don't reject correction or you*
> *will certainly wander from the ways of truth."*
> —Proverbs 19:27 *TPT*

167

You are my one, holy and true. You are my one I always look to. Lord, help me forgive and see this life I have is bought by Thee. Help me to see with eyes of glory. Help me to speak fluently. Help me to hear and not just see. Help me to love like Your heart is in me. Help me, Father, please help me.

> "But now, O Yahweh-God, make yourself real
> to me like You promised me You would. Because
> of Your constant love and Your heart-melting
> kindness, come be my hero and deliver me!"
>
> —Psalms 109:21 *TPT*

168

Lord, You know my heart. You know my ways. Why do I struggle and not sing Your praise? Why do I sink into a deep dark pit? Why do You come after me and tell me to repent? Why do I deserve this love that You give? Why, Father, why did You die so I could live?

> *"By day the Lord directs His love, at night His song is with me—a prayer to the God of my life."*
>
> **—Psalms 42:8** *NIV*

169

Fighting to stay strong. Fighting to be here. Fighting to stay and not live in fear. Fighting for my beliefs. Fighting for Your ways. Fighting, oh fighting. Soon you will not stay. Break down the walls and insecurities. Break them down and have so much peace. He has not called us to fight, but surrender and win. He leads us to be triumphant.

> "For God is the triumphant King; all the powers of the earth are His. So, sing your celebration songs of highest praise to the glorious Enlightened One!"
>
> –Psalms 47:7 *TPT*

170

He says, fight the good fight of faith. It seems so hard and the enemy tries to take. Go fight the good fight of faith. Flesh be gone. Spirit rise and say, I rule over you and this I will take. Never will I bow down in fear or dismay. This faith I have will live and never die. Jesus, oh Jesus, you are my why.

> *"So, fight with faith for the winner's prize! Lay your hands upon eternal life, to which you were called and about which you made the good confession before the multitude of witnesses!"*
>
> −1 Timothy 6:12 *TPT*

171

Hey, Jesus, it's me talking here. Where do You go when I'm lonely and scared? I hear Him say, I'm right here, surrender to me and cast those cares.

> "casting all your care upon Him,
> for He cares for you."
>
> −1 Peter 5:7 *NKJV*

172

It's time to shine. It's time to reap. You have planted and sown many seeds. It's time to reap. It's time to share. Your Father will bless. Oh, He cares.

> "Then He said to His disciples, 'The harvest is [indeed] plentiful, but the workers are few.'"
>
> –Matthew 9:37 *AMP*

173

Lord, You called me to dream. You called me to be. You say it's coming. You say to believe. How long shall I wait? How long will this take? I'm hurting inside with every breath that I take. I know, like I know Your word is spoken and true, but Lord, please help me wait peacefully with You.

> *"But those who wait for the Lord [who expect, look for, and hope in Him] Will gain new strength and renew their power; They will lift up their wings [and rise up close to God] like eagles [rising toward the sun]; They will run and not become weary, They will walk and not grow tired."*
>
> –Isaiah 40:31 *AMP*

174

How can you feel so low? Walking, talking, loving Jesus and be in such a funk, a mood like He has not called us to do life like this. Wake up from your pitiful mess, shake it off and request that power He holds. Take back control. Live again. Love and be His.

> "He lifted me out of the pit of despair, out of the mud and the mire. He set my feet on solid ground and steadied me as I walked along."
>
> —Psalms 40:2 *NLT*

175

Crying tears. Fighting fears. Where does this come within? Where does it come from? Oh, it's Him. He gives us the power to fight and overcome. That power we hold. The power we seek only comes from Him, the humble and meek Lord. Awake me from my sleep. Don't let me stay and weep. Hold me up. Hold me there. Cast all my cares. You are the one I choose. I will walk this life with You. This I will do, because I know then I will never lose.

> "I also pray that you will understand the incredible greatness of God's power for us who believe him. This is the same mighty power."
>
> –Ephesians 1:19 *NLT*

176

Trials. Temptation. This we will have. It says in the Bible, your hearts be glad. I have overcome this world you see. Have the faith. Have the hope one day you will be living here in eternity, if you choose with me.

> "These things I have spoken to you, that in me you may have peace. In the world you will have tribulation; but be of good cheer, I have overcome the world.'"
>
> –John 16:33 *NKJV*

177

The flesh is a beast. It makes me want all these evil things. Die flesh. I say not today, will I stray, Holy Spirit. We have the power to overcome. Ask the Holy Spirit. He won.

> "For if you live according to the flesh, you will die;
> but if by the Spirit you put to death the misdeeds
> of the body, you will live."
>
> —Romans 8:13 *NIV*

178

Joy. Happiness. All of these things. We are called to live and walk through pain even with our trials ahead. We are called to be joyful, instead. Help me, Father, live in the spirit and see this is possible when You are leading me.

> *"Yet I will [choose to] rejoice in the Lord; I will [choose to] shout in exultation in the [victorious] God of my salvation!"*
>
> –Habakkuk 3:18 *AMP*

179

Holy Ghost, you have a home in me. This home feels power and victory. Holy Ghost, You give me peace. I feel it almost instantly. Holy Ghost, You help me discern, give me knowledge and wisdom, it's true. Holy Ghost, my best friend. That's You. The joy and laughter You bring. My spirit jumps and sings. Oh, how did I ever not choose You? You awaken me with truth. Thank you for being a friend. Thank You. I always have the power to overcome with You guiding and being the One.

> *"Create in me a clean heart, O God,*
> *And renew a steadfast spirit within me."*
> —Psalms 51:10 *NKJV*

180

The hurting. The lost. I see them on the streets, at the grocery store, and they are so weak, dead, and broken. I see them, Lord, and not a word spoken. What gets someone so low? What can't they see? What don't they know? Will you show? Somethings I will never understand, but I know you always have a plan. So, I pray and walk away, knowing it's You Father that saves.

> *"He won't brush aside the bruised and broken. He will be gentle with the weak and feeble, until His victory releases justice."*
>
> –Matthew 12:20 *TPT*

181

Cuts. Words thrown. Shallow remarks and burns. Oh, how easy it is to live this way, with no responsibility or shame. Father, awake the spirit. Give the desire to choose, to live, surrender to You, be convicted and change with truth. Let the enemy not touch and fill with lies. You won over him. That's our prize. Today, I ask if anyone is struggling this way, they humble themselves, seek and pray. Be filled with Your Spirit and say thank you, Jesus, for showing me the way, for giving me life. I choose to stay the path You write. Help me forgive me of my sins. I want to follow You. I truly repent.

"And don't get drunk with wine, which is rebellion; instead, be filled continually with the Holy Spirit."

–Ephesians 5:18 *TPT*

182

My children, oh, how I love them. Your children, I know I give them to You and truly let go. They are Yours. Given to me. A precious blessing. Oh, how I see. Oh, the peace I have when I place these children in Your hands. Oh, the joy these children bring. Thank You, Father, for choosing me.

"Children are God's love-gift;
they are heaven's generous reward."

—Psalms 127:3 *TPT*

183

Time away. People say I need time away, but what do you truly need, time away or Jesus? You see there's a void there that can only be filled, only be filled by the One that loves us. Still that void never truly goes away until you live for Jesus and choose to follow and not stray. Today, I say ask Him to live in you. Stay, keep and love you. You will be whole and renewed if you dare to simply choose.

> "Then Jesus said to His disciples, 'If any of you wants to be my follower, you must give up your own way, take up your cross, and follow me.'"
>
> –Matthew 16:24 *NLT*

184

The world. The flesh is simply a mess. It comes. It breaks. It sees evil and shame. This world has dug into the pits of hell and I have a feeling it knows full well choices, excuses, blindness causes this. Not looking to heaven. Our Father that loves us, help us, wake us from our sleep. Shake us. This world. This flesh. I do not see. Repent. Repent. Turn from your ways. Repent. Repent. It's a brand-new day. Oh, the joy He gives us to take. Oh, the joy in that sweet surrender I say. Oh, the joy you could have if you say, Jesus I'm sorry, help me live in a new way.

> "Come back to your senses as you ought, and stop sinning; for there are some who are ignorant of God—I say this to your shame."
>
> –1 Corinthians 15:34 *NIV*

185

Be well and be saved. Be well, be saved. Be well, be saved. Be well, be saved. Be well, be saved. Be well, be saved. Be well, be saved. Be well, be saved. Be well, be saved. Be well, be saved. Be well, be saved. Be well, be saved. Be well, be saved. Be well, be saved. Be well, be saved. Be well, be saved. Let go of the ill, rise up and feel.

> *"But everyone who calls on the name of the Lord will be saved."*
>
> —Acts 2:21 *TPT*

186

Let go, let go of the HOW and TO DO. Let go, let go and be faithful and true. Let go, and let me take the lead. Let go, my child and believe. Let go, my plan has been set. Let go, live each day as there is nothing left. Let go, my child and believe. Let go, it's just ME. If you find me you will find everything. I will lead I will guide. Take your focus take your pride, let it die to self. Live fully for me. Endurance and peace this shall bring. Open up I'm pouring out. Let's conquer this life I'm rooting for YOU.

Let go and win.

187

I am done with this chapter; I am moving on. I am done with this chapter; I am moving on. Thank You for this season, thank You for this gift. I am done with this chapter, never shall I miss all You have given me in each chapter, each season. I have grown to be wise and free.

Thank You for this chapter.

ABOUT THE AUTHOR

I believe it's the Father, the Son, and the Holy Ghost, and everything else flows from it. I have an amazing husband, Justin, of fifteen years. I have two precious daughters that make my world go round. Addie, 14 and Liv, 9. We reside in Bourbon, MO and founded True Love Ministries. My heart is to flow from the heart of Jesus and tell the world the relationship with our Father is the most important of all.